Our Values

CARING FOR EARTH

By Steffi Cavell-Clarke

Crabtree Publishing Company

www.crabtreebooks.com

1-800-387-7650

Published in Canada
Crabtree Publishing
616 Welland Avenue
St. Catharines, ON
L2M 5V6

Published in the United States
Crabtree Publishing
PMB 59051
350 Fifth Ave, 59th Floor
New York, NY 10118

Published by Crabtree Publishing Company in 2018

First Published by Book Life in 2018
Copyright © 2018 Book Life

Author: Steffi Cavell-Clarke

Editors: Kirsty Holmes, Janine Deschenes

Design: Daniel Scase

Proofreader: Petrice Custance

Production coordinator and
 prepress technician (interior): Margaret Amy Salter

Prepress technician (covers): Ken Wright

Print coordinator: Margaret Amy Salter

Photographs
Abbreviations: l – left, r –right, b – bottom, t – top, c-centre, m – middle. Images are courtesy of Shutterstock.com. With thanks to Getty Images, Thinkstock Photo and iStockphoto. Front cover – wavebreakmedia. 2 & 3l – Sunny Studio. 4 – Rawpixel. com. 5: tl – Monkey Business Images, tm – Tom Wang, tr – Yuliya Evstratenko, mr – Romrodphoto, br – Luis Molinero, bm – Pressmaster, bl – amenic181, ml – ESB Professional. 6 – Oksana Kuzmina, 7 – wavebreakmedia. 8 – Anna Nahabed, 9 – Yuliya Evstratenko, 10 – Hung Chung Chih, 11: t – INSAGO, m – branislavpudar, b – De Visu. 12 – Toa55. 13 – SimplyDay. 14 – 2xSamara.com. 15 – Nikola Solev. 16 – wavebreakmedia. 17 – Rawpixel.com. 18 – Onyx9. 19 – Mny-Jhee. 20 – Sunny Studio. 21 – Rawpixel.com. 22 – Rawpixel.com. 23: tl – Brian A Jackson, tm – wavebreakmedia, tr – Switlana Symonenko, br – Africa Studio, bl – TonnaPong

Printed in the USA/012018/BG20171102

Library and Archives Canada Cataloguing in Publication

Cavell-Clarke, Steffi, author
    Caring for Earth / Steffi Cavell-Clarke.

(Our values)
Includes index.
Issued in print and electronic formats.
ISBN 978-0-7787-4729-1 (hardcover).--
ISBN 978-0-7787-4744-4 (softcover).--
ISBN 978-1-4271-2082-3 (HTML)

    1. Environmental management--Juvenile literature. 2. Environmentalism--Juvenile literature. 3. Environmental protection--Juvenile literature. 4. Community life--Environmental aspects--Juvenile literature. I. Title.

GE195.5.C38 2018   j333.72   C2017-906919-5
                                          C2017-906920-9

Library of Congress Cataloging-in-Publication Data

CIP available at the Library of Congress

CONTENTS

Words that are bolded, like **this,** can be found in the glossary on page 24.

WHAT ARE VALUES?

Values are the things that you believe are important, such as celebrating different beliefs. The ways we think and behave depend on our values. They help us learn how to **respect** each other and ourselves. Sharing the same values as others helps us live and work together in a **community**.

Being responsible

Making good choices

Making friends

Our Values

Caring for the environment

Listening to others

Helping others

5

CARING FOR EARTH

Planet Earth is home to seven billion people. All those people need food, clean water, and shelter to survive. We get everything we need to survive from Earth, so it's important that we care for it and make it a healthy place to live.

Caring for Earth means doing things that will help to keep the environment on our planet healthy, such as recycling plastic bottles and turning off lights when they are not needed. An environment is the sourroundings in which we live.

WHY IS IT IMPORTANT?

Planet Earth has the **natural resources** that we need to survive. We depend on water to drink, land to grow food, and clean air to breathe. We also use natural resources such as oil, gas, and wind energy to power our cars, homes, and schools.

Wind energy creates **electricity**, which can power our homes.

Some natural resources, such as trees, are renewable. This means that they can be replaced over time. Others, such as oil, are non-renewable. They cannot be replaced. It is important to save Earth's resources so there will be enough for people in the future to use.

We should try not to waste Earth's resources.

POLLUTION

Humans, animals, and plants need a healthy environment to live in. Pollution makes environments unsafe. It happens when harmful substances are introduced into land, water, or air. Pollution can harm humans, animals, and plants.

Air pollution is when the air has been **contaminated** by smoke or harmful **gases**.

Land pollution is when Earth's surface has been contaminated by **waste** or damaged by humans.

Water pollution is when water has been contaminated by waste or harmful substances, such as oil.

CLEAN AIR

Air pollution is very dangerous to animals, humans, and plants. One of the biggest causes of air pollution is the burning of **fossil fuels** and the gases given out by cars and airplanes.

Jordan learned that when his parents drove him to his coding club, their car polluted the air. He decided to bike to club meetings instead. Jordan also told his friends about air pollution. They agreed to bike to the club with him. Jordan's choice shows that he cares for Earth's environment.

FRESH WATER

Water covers most of planet Earth. Oceans and seas have salt water, and rivers and lakes have fresh water. People need to drink fresh water to stay alive and healthy. Fresh water can be polluted when waste is put into it. This harms us, and the plants and animals who live in water.

We should never throw garbage or any kind of waste into the water.

There is only a small amount of clean, fresh water on Earth, so it is important to save water where we can. Here are some simple ways we can help:

- Never leave water running. Turn off the tap while you brush your teeth or wash your hands.

- Take a shower instead of a bath

- Ask an adult to fix dripping taps or other water leaks

15

RECYCLING

Garbage is made up of things that we no longer want or need. We create huge amounts of garbage every day. It is either buried or burned, which is harmful to the environment. To help reduce the amount of garbage we create, we can recycle some types of garbage, such as paper, plastic, glass, and metal.

Recycling is when old things are turned into new things.

WE RECYCLE

We can also help the environment by reducing the amount of garbage that we create. We can do this by using reusable bags, containers, and water bottles. We can also ask our parents to buy things that do not come in a lot of plastic packaging.

By bringing her food to school in reusable containers, Melissa does not create any garbage at lunch time.

CARING FOR WILDLIFE

There are many animal **species** that are endangered, which means they are in danger of becoming **extinct**. This is because humans are destroying their habitats, or homes, in order to access more natural resources.

Mountain gorillas are an endangered species. They are at risk because of habitat loss and hunting.

Humans cut down trees and use the wood to make paper, furniture, and buildings. This leaves the animals who live in the trees without a home. We can help fix this problem by volunteering to plant trees, or supporting a **charity** that plants trees around the world.

CARING FOR EACH OTHER

When you help keep the environment clean and healthy, you show you care about other people, plants, and animals. It is important to do our best to help all living things on Earth be safe and healthy.

Abby and her friends noticed that there was litter in the yard at their school. They learned that their classmates left their water bottles outside during recess. To help fix this problem, they decided to collect water bottles after recess. They encouraged their classmates to recycle to keep the school environment clean and healthy.

MAKING A DIFFERENCE

It is important to care for the environment where you live. There are lots of things we can do where we live that will help all of planet Earth.

Recycle and reuse
when you can

Walk or bike instead
of riding in a car

Always put
your garbage
in a can. Do
not litter.

Remember these simple ways to help
make a difference to your environment:

Switch off electrical things,
such as lights, when they
are not in use

Save water by
turning off taps

GLOSSARY

charity [CHAR-i-tee] An organization that helps those in need

community [kuh-MYOO-ni-tee] A group of people who live, work, and play in a place

contaminated [kuh n-TAM-uh-neyt-ed] Something made unclean by adding a poisonous or polluting substance to it

electricity [ih-lek-TRIS-i-tee] A form of energy that we use to power our homes and buildings

environment [en-VAHY-ruh n muh nt] Your surroundings

extinct [ik-STINGKT] No longer alive

fossil fuels [FOS-uh l FYOO-uh l] Fuels, such as coal, oil and gas, that formed millions of years ago

gases [gases] Air-like substances that expand freely to fill any space

natural resources [NACH-er-uh l REE-sawrs] Useful materials created by nature

respect [ri-SPEKT] Giving something or someone the attention it deserves

responsible [ri-spon-suh-buhl] Reliable or dependable

species [SPEE-sheez] A group of very similar animals that are capable of producing young together

waste [weyst] Unwanted things

INDEX